Elena Kats-Chernin

Kwong Song

for solo piano

2007

BB 3335

Kwong Song

for solo piano

ELENA KATS-CHERNIN

Slow ♩ = 92

26th April 2007
Coogee, Sydney

Programme Notes

In 2006 when my good friend, celebrated Australian chef Kylie Kwong's father was gravely ill, I wrote a piece Kwong Song for her, in which I tried to express the sorrow of the imminent loss of someone close and try to foreshadow the memory of that someone. It is, like Blue Silence, quite minimal in its material and is quietly repetitive. The initial idea was to write a succession of small short sighs, this grew into a kind of waltz. There are versions of this piece for a) string quartet, b) clarinet quartet and c) flute trio (or flute and piano).

ELENA KATS-CHERNIN

Kwong Song
for solo piano

(2007)

www.boosey.com

AN IMAGEM COMPANY

BB 3335

ISMN 979-0-2025-3335-2
ISBN 978-3-7931-4017-7